KU-180-646

07/05

WOJ

07. MAR 07

21. MAY 07

14. APR 08

15. OCT 1.

Last copy.

WOODSIDE LIBRARY
TEL 484534
....
PLEASE RETURN TO THE ABOVE LIBRARY OR ANY OTHER ABERDEEN
CITY LIBRARY, ON OR BEFORE THE DUE DATE. TO RENEW, PLEASE
QUOTE THE DUE DATE AND THE BARCODE NUMBER.

Aberdeen City Council
Library & Information Services

WITHDRAWN

X000 000 016 3239

ABERDEEN CITY LIB.

What's it Like?

Down Syndrome

Angela Royston

www.heinemann.co.uk/library

Visit our website to find out more information about **Heinemann Library** books.

To order:

 Phone 44 (0) 1865 888066

Send a fax to 44 (0) 1865 314091

 Visit the Heinemann Bookshop at www.heinemann.co.uk/library to browse our catalogue and order online.

First published in Great Britain by Heinemann Library, Halley Court, Jordan Hill, Oxford OX2 8EJ, part of Harcourt Education.
Heinemann is a registered trademark of Harcourt Education Ltd.

© Harcourt Education Ltd 2005
The moral right of the proprietor has been asserted.

All rights reserved. No part of this publication may be reproduced, stored in a retrieval system, or transmitted in any form or by any means, electronic, mechanical, photocopying, recording, or otherwise, without either the prior written permission of the publishers or a licence permitting restricted copying in the United Kingdom issued by the Copyright Licensing Agency Ltd, 90 Tottenham Court Road, London W1T 4LP (www.cla.co.uk).

Editorial: Sarah Shannon and Richard Woodham
Design: Ron Kamen, Victoria Bevan and Celia Jones
Picture Research: Maria Joannou and Kay Altwegg
Production: Amanda Meaden

Originated by Dot Gradations Ltd
Printed and bound in China by South China Printing Company

ISBN 0 431 11226 6
09 08 07 06 05
10 9 8 7 6 5 4 3 2 1

British Library Cataloguing in Publication Data
Royston, Angela
 Down Syndrome – (What's it like?)
 362.1'96858842

A full catalogue record for this book is available from the British Library.

Acknowledgements
The publishers would like to thank the following for permission to reproduce photographs:
Alamy p.10 (Laura Dwight); Bubbles Picture Library p.17 (Angela Hampton); Corbis pp.21 (Ricki Rosen), 26 (Stephanie Maze); John Birdsall Social Issues Library pp.20, 25; Mencap pp. 22 (Martin Sookias), 27 (Martin Sookias); Reuters p.11; Rex Features p.29 (Phanie Agency); Science Photo Library pp. 4 (Lauren Shear), 5 (Lauren Shear), 6 (Lauren Shear), 7 (Lauren Shear), 12 (Hattie Young), 14 (Lauren Shear), 16 (Hattie Young), 19 (Lauren Shear); Shout pp.13 (John Callan), 18 (John Callan), 23 (John Callan), 28 (John Callan); The Down's Syndrome Association (Lauren Shear) pp.8, 9, 15, 24.

Cover photograph of a boy with Down Syndrome playing with friends at a mainstream school reproduced with permission of Science Photo Library/Lauren Shear.

We would like to thank Marie Benton for her assistance in the preparation of this book.

Every effort has been made to contact copyright holders of any material reproduced in this book. Any omissions will be rectified in subsequent printings if notice is given to the publishers.

The paper used to print this book comes from sustainable resources.

362 . 1968588

Contents

Words appearing in the text in bold, **like this**, are explained in the Glossary.

 Find out more about what it's like to have Down syndrome at www.heinemannexplore.co.uk

What is Down syndrome?

Down syndrome is a **condition** that some people are born with. People with Down syndrome are **affected** in different ways.

This person has Down syndrome.

Down syndrome is not an illness. You cannot catch Down syndrome from someone who has it.

Who has Down syndrome?

Doctors carry out special tests to tell if a baby or child has Down syndrome or not. This baby has Down syndrome.

These children are brother and sister.

In some families, one child may have Down syndrome but the other children do not.

Like everyone else

In most ways people with Down syndrome are just like everyone else. Sometimes they need a little more help than people who do not have Down syndrome.

8

People with Down syndrome may feel
happy, sad, or left out. They play with
other children and make good friends
with them.

Learning

Children with Down syndrome do not learn as quickly as most other children. They usually learn to walk and talk later than most children do.

This young boy is enjoying walking on his own.

Doing something is the best way to learn about it.

People with Down syndrome **understand** more easily when they can see something. They find it harder to learn by just **listening**.

Moving

Babies born with Down syndrome may be slow to begin moving their **muscles**. Some babies are given special **exercises** that make them kick their legs.

Special exercises strengthen the baby's muscles.

As they grow older and stronger,
children with Down syndrome can
do the same things as other children.

This girl is good
at jumping on
a **trampoline**.

Speaking

Young children with Down syndrome often find it hard to remember words. They sometimes use hand signals as well as words to help make themselves clear when speaking to other people.

This boy is using his hands to describe what something looks like.

Children with Down syndrome usually **understand** much more than they can say. They sometimes get **frustrated** because they cannot always think of the words they want to use.

Reading and writing

Most children with Down syndrome learn to read like other children, but it may take them a year or two longer.

Children with Down syndrome may take longer to learn to write and count. They may need lots of help while learning to write and count.

This girl with Down syndrome is learning to write with the rest of the class.

Extra help

Some children with Down syndrome go to special schools. Here they learn with other children who need extra help to learn.

Many children with Down syndrome go to ordinary schools. A **classroom assistant** may sometimes help them with their work.

Seeing and hearing

Many people need glasses to help them see properly. People with Down syndrome are more likely to need glasses. Not all people with Down syndrome need them.

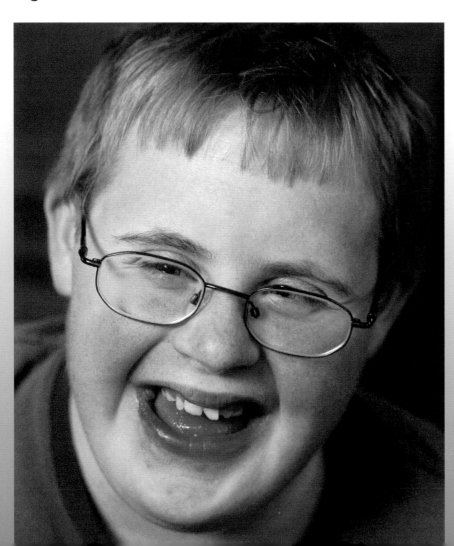

These children find it difficult to hear.

People with Down syndrome are more likely to have problems hearing than children born without the **condition**. Many of these problems can be corrected using **eardrops** or **hearing aids**.

Remembering things

Many people with Down syndrome find it hard to remember things they have been told. It is much easier to remember something if it is written down.

People with Down syndrome often write things down to help them remember — just like people who write a shopping list to remind them what to buy.

Having fun

People with Down syndrome enjoy the same things as everyone else. For example, they enjoy eating out and going to the cinema.

A person with Down syndrome may
enjoy the same games and sports as
everyone else. They may also enjoy
playing a musical instrument.

Living without help

When they grow up, people with Down syndrome may choose to live in their own home. They may cook and look after themselves. Some marry and have children.

This man has Down syndrome. He is using the internet to look after his bank account.

Some people with Down syndrome like to live where there are people to help them. Others live with their parents or family.

Working

People with Down syndrome do many different jobs. Some might be **photographers**, while others might work in offices or shops.

This person is working in a restaurant.

This person is making nesting boxes for birds.

Some people with Down syndrome work for **organizations** that provide jobs and extra help for people who need it. For example, this person is working in a craft shop.

Find out more

The Down's Syndrome Association
This organisation provides help and information for people who have Down syndrome, and their families.
www.downs-syndrome.org.uk

National Down Syndrome Society
This website contains lots of information about Down syndrome, and shows you how you can take part in raising money for people with the condition.
www.ndss.org

Down Syndrome New South Wales – Australia
Click on 'Stories' to read about the lives of people who have Down syndrome.
www.dsansw.org.au

 Find out more about what it's like to have Down syndrome at www.heinemannexplore.co.uk

Disclaimer
All the internet addresses (URLs) given in this book were valid at the time of going to press. However, due to the dynamic nature of the Internet, some addresses may have changed, or sites may have ceased to exist since publication. While the author and publishers regret any inconvenience this may cause readers, no responsibility for any such changes can be accepted by either the author or the publishers.

Glossary

affected changed in some way

classroom assistant person who helps a teacher or some of the children in the classroom

condition something that affects the way some parts of your body work

eardrops medicine that is dropped into your ear to help you hear more clearly

exercises particular ways of moving parts of your body to make your muscles, bones or joints stronger

frustrated feeling angry because you are unable to do what you want to

hearing aid machine that can help people hear more clearly

listen pay attention to something that you can hear

muscles one of the parts of the body that gives it the power to move

organization group of people who work together for a purpose

photographer someone who takes photographs

trampoline bouncy frame that lets you jump very high

understand know what something means

More books to read

Powell, Jillian, *Luke has Down Syndrome* (Evans Brothers, 2004)

Gordon, Melanie, *Let's Talk about Down Syndrome* (PowerKids Press, 2003)

Index

ABERDEEN
CITY
LIBRARIES

Titles in the What's It Like? series include:

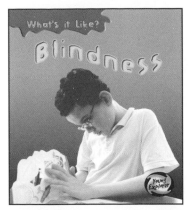

Hardback   0 431 11223 1

Hardback   0 431 11225 8

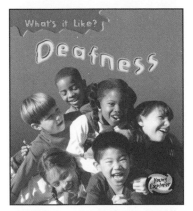

Hardback   0 431 11222 3

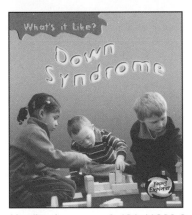

Hardback   0 431 11226 6

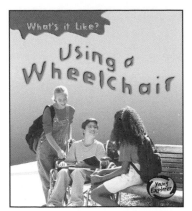

Hardback   0 431 11224 X

Find out about the other titles in this series on our website www.heinemann.co.uk/library